First Facts®

UNEXPLAINED MYSTERIES

The Unsolved Mystery of

UFOS

by Terri Sievert

CAPSTONE PRESS
a capstone imprint

First Facts are published by Capstone Press,
1710 Roe Crest Drive, North Mankato, Minnesota 56003
www.capstonepub.com

Library of Congress Cataloging-in-Publication Data

Sievert, Terri.
The unsolved mystery of UFOs / by Terri Sievert.
p. cm. — (First facts. Unexplained mysteries)
Includes bibliographical references and index.
Summary: "Presents the mystery of UFOs, including current theories and famous examples"—
Provided by publisher.
ISBN 978-1-62065-135-3 (library binding)
ISBN 978-1-62065-812-3 (paperback)
ISBN 978-1-4765-1067-5 (eBook PDF)
1. Unidentified flying objects—Juvenile literature. I. Title.
TL789.2.S543 2013
001.942—dc23
2012028441

Editorial Credits

Mari Bolte, editor; Veronica Correia, designer; Wanda Winch, media researcher;
Jennifer Walker, production specialist

Photo Credits

Alamy: Mary Evans Picture Library, 12; Corbis: Bettmann, 15; Courtesy of Larry Elmore 4,
Courtesy of www.ufocasebook.com, 10–11; Getty Images Inc: AFP/USAF, 7; Shutterstock: Aaron
Rutten, 8, Andrea Danti, 20–21, Jennifer Gottschalk, (abstract disc design), 1 Martin Capek, purple
nebula, oorka, cover, sad, 16, tr3gin, 18, zeber, background

Table of Contents

An Object in the Sky

July 4, 1947, was a day the people of Roswell, New Mexico would never forget. That day, a strange, bright object fell from the sky.

Two men rushed to the crash site. There, they saw pieces of a bat-shaped ship with narrow wings. They also said they saw the bodies of **aliens**.

alien—a creature not from Earth

Other people saw the bodies too. Some said the aliens had four fingers, no hair, and white skin. Others said the aliens had big heads and large black eyes.

The U.S. Army Air Force cleaned up the wreck. Officials originally said they'd found a flying disc. The next day, they said the wreck was part of a weather balloon. But many believe that an alien spaceship crashed in the desert.

Many people believe the alien bodies were stored in **Hangar** 84 at Roswell Army Air Field.

hangar—a large building where airplanes are parked

A service member from Roswell Army Air Field with pieces of the spaceship

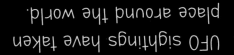

UFO sightings have taken
place around the world.

Chapter
2

History and Legend

Strange objects in the sky have been reported since **ancient** times. In 329 BC, Alexander the Great wrote about an unidentified flying object (UFO) sighting. He said that two silver flying objects shot fire at his army.

Some people think aliens made the large stone statues on Easter Island. Others think they built Great Britain's Stonehenge.

ancient—from a long time ago

On October 18, 1973, a helicopter flew over Mansfield, Ohio. The men in the helicopter saw a gray, oval-shaped object in the sky. It flew toward them so fast they thought it would hit the helicopter. The spaceship had a rounded top and a red light on its front. The underside of the ship glowed green, and a white light lit its back.

11

About 3 million people in the United States believe they have had a close encounter with aliens.

In 1961 Betty and Barney Hill noticed a colorful spacecraft following their car. Barney said he saw figures in the ship. They heard a beeping sound and began to feel sleepy.

When the couple woke up, they were in a different place. Their car had strange marks all over it. Betty learned the local Air Force base had been tracking a strange object in the area. While under **hypnosis**, the couple remembered that they had been aboard a UFO.

hypnosis—a method used to put people in a sleeplike state

Chapter 3

UFO or Not?

Are aliens really out there? Some people say no way. Others want to believe that we're not alone in the **universe**. Sometimes new types of planes are mistaken for UFOs. Weather balloons and lights have also been thought to be UFOs. These objects are called identified flying objects (IFOs.)

universe—everything that exists, including Earth, the planets, the stars, and all of space

About 70,000 UFOs are reported each year. There are about 192 sightings each day.

Chapter 4

Searching for UFOs

UFO hunters look at **evidence** to learn more about these strange objects. They collect pictures, drawings, and videos. But nobody has proven that UFOs are real.

True or False?

Are UFOs real?

True:
The U.S. Air Force studied more than 12,000 UFO sightings between 1948 and 1969. The study was called Project Blue Book.

False:
The Air Force decided that UFOs were either natural objects or **hoaxes**. Project Blue Book has never been reopened.

True:
There have been hundreds of UFO sightings around the world.

False:
Many things are mistaken for UFOs. Mistaken objects include sunlight reflecting off ice crystals, birds' wings, **mirages**, and marsh gas.

True:
Alien spacecrafts have been recovered from crash sites or photographed.

False:
Many of the crashes and photos turned out to be fake.

evidence—information, items, and facts that help prove something to be true or false
hoax—a trick to make people believe something that is not true
mirage—something that appears to be there but is not

The Nazca Lines in Peru show lines, shapes, and pictures of plants and animals.

UFOs have been seen around the world for thousands of years. Cave drawings show objects that look like UFOs. Ancient writings tell of shapes flying through the air.

Were these strange
objects created by aliens?

Crop Circles

True:
Crop circles usually appear overnight. They are often circular and large enough to be caused by a spaceship.

False:
People have been caught making crop circles.

Stonehenge

True:
This huge stone monument is shaped like a UFO. No one is sure how the stone circle was formed or why.

False:
There are other stone circles throughout Great Britain. Today researchers believe people could have moved the stones.

Nazca Lines

True:
These huge drawings located in Peru were created between 500 BC and AD 500. Some believe they were ancient runways for alien spacecraft.

False:
Researchers have shown that the drawings are easy to copy. If UFOs had landed on top of them, the drawings would have been disturbed.

Could there be life on other planets? Some people believe aliens exist. They think that people aren't alone in the universe. Others need to see it to believe it. Maybe someday the mystery of UFOs will be solved.

alien (AY-lee-uhn)—a creature not from Earth

ancient (AYN-shunt)—from a long time ago

evidence (EV-uh-duhnss)—information, items, and facts that help prove something to be true or false

hangar (HANG-ur)—a large building where airplanes are parked

hoax (HOHKS)—a trick to make people believe something that is not true

hypnosis (hip-NOH-siss)—a method used to put people in a sleeplike state in which they answer questions and easily respond to different suggestions

mirage (muh-RAZH)—something that appears to be there but is not

universe (YOO-nuh-verss)—everything that exists, including Earth, the planets, the the stars, and all of space

Polydoros, Lori. *Top 10 UFO and Alien Mysteries.* Top 10 Unexplained. North Mankato, Minn.: Capstone Press, 2012.

Walker, Kathryn. *Mysteries of UFOs.* Unsolved! New York: Crabtree Pub., 2009.

Wencel, Dave. *UFOs.* The Unexplained. Minneapolis: Bellwether Media, 2011.

Internet Sites

FactHound offers a safe, fun way to find Internet sites related to this book. All of the sites on FactHound have been researched by our staff.

Here's all you do:

Visit *www.facthound.com*

Type in this code: 9781620651353

Super-cool stuff! Check out projects, games and lots more at
www.capstonekids.com